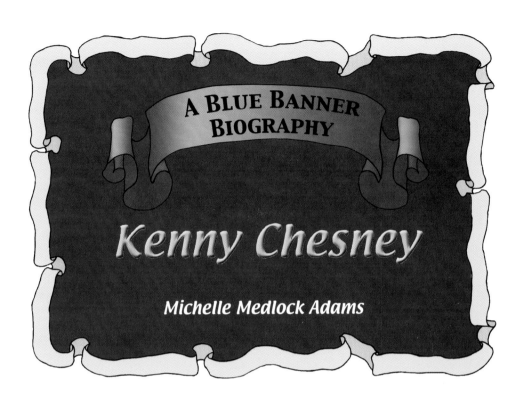

A BLUE BANNER
BIOGRAPHY

Kenny Chesney

Michelle Medlock Adams

Mitchell Lane
PUBLISHERS
P.O. Box 196
Hockessin, Delaware 19707
Visit us on the web: www.mitchelllane.com
Comments? email us: mitchelllane@mitchelllane.com

Printing   1   2   3   4   5   6   7   8   9

Blue Banner Biographies

Alan Jackson	Alicia Keys	Allen Iverson
Ashanti	Ashlee Simpson	Ashton Kutcher
Avril Lavigne	Bernie Mac	Beyoncé
Bow Wow	Britney Spears	Christina Aguilera
Christopher Paul Curtis	Clay Aiken	Condoleezza Rice
Daniel Radcliffe	Derek Jeter	Eminem
Eve	50 Cent	Gwen Stefani
Ice Cube	Jamie Foxx	Ja Rule
Jay-Z	Jennifer Lopez	J. K. Rowling
Jodie Foster	Justin Berfield	Kate Hudson
Kelly Clarkson	**Kenny Chesney**	Lance Armstrong
Lindsay Lohan	Mariah Carey	Mario
Mary-Kate and Ashley Olsen	Melissa Gilbert	Michael Jackson
Miguel Tejada	Missy Elliott	Nelly
Orlando Bloom	P. Diddy	Paris Hilton
Peyton Manning	Queen Latifah	Rita Williams-Garcia
Ritchie Valens	Ron Howard	Rudy Giuliani
Sally Field	Selena	Shirley Temple
Tim McGraw	Usher	

Library of Congress Cataloging-in-Publication Data
Adams, Michelle Medlock.
     Kenny Chesney/by Michelle Medlock Adams.
        p. cm. — (Blue banner biographies)
     Includes bibliographical references, discography, and index.
     ISBN 1-58415-502-7 (library bound: alk paper)
        1. Chesney, Kenny — Juvenile literature. 2. Country musicians — United States —
Biography — Juvenile literature. I. Title. II. Series. Blue banner biography.
ML3930.C448A32 2006
782.421642092 — dc22
    [B]   2005036690
ISBN–10: 1-58415-502-7   ISBN–13: 978-158415-502-7

ABOUT THE AUTHOR: Earning first-place awards from Associated Press, the Hoosier State Press Association, and the Society of Professional Journalists, Michelle Medlock Adams has published more than 3,000 articles in newspapers and magazines around the country, such as *Writer's Digest*, *Today's Christian Woman*, *Brio*, and *American Cheerleader Magazine*. She has also authored 26 books, including her award-winning picture book, *Conversations On the Ark*. She and her husband, Jeff, and their two daughters, Abby and Allyson, live in Texas with their three miniature dachshunds.

PLB

CONTENTS

Kenny Chesney sings to his loyal fan following on June 13, 2002, at the 31st Annual Fan Fair event in Nashville, Tennessee. This four-day country music festival is the world's largest of its kind, featuring concerts, fan clubs, parties, and lots of chances to mix and mingle with country music's biggest stars.

Small-Town Superstar

*A*s Kenny Chesney looked out over the sea of screaming fans on July 30, 2005, he couldn't believe his eyes. There were more than 54,000 people packed into Heinz Field in Pittsburgh, Pennsylvania, and they were all there to see his concert. It was the largest crowd to ever attend a country concert in Pittsburgh.

Not only that, there was a TV crew on hand to tape the concert—footage that would make up Chesney's first network TV special, which would air on ABC on November 23, 2005. And why not? As the Academy of Country Music's and Country Music Association's Entertainer of the Year, Chesney was the perfect guy for a prime-time, hourlong special.

Chesney wasn't about to let that TV special happen if he couldn't help direct it. He wanted to make sure the show would respect the friendship with his fans that he had developed and cherished, and he wanted to give those fans an inside look at what life was really like from the road.

Of course, no story or special about Kenny Chesney would be complete without including footage of the Caribbean island where he goes to relax and think. After all, many of his songs were birthed in a boat or on the beach, so the island holds a special place in his heart. He has always loved the ocean and the beach. They have been an important part of his life since he was a little kid vacationing with his family. He wanted his fans to share that love with him.

He has always loved the ocean and the beach. They have been an important part of his life since he was a little kid.

"I always believed that there was something more to it, whether it was religion or something else," Chesney shared in an interview posted on bnarecords.com online. "I always felt whatever that is more when I was on the ocean. I always felt more something, and I didn't quite know what it was—just that it made me feel better, more settled."

As he worked on the TV special, sharing his soul with millions of viewers, he couldn't help thinking back to a time when the only audience he had consisted of a few homeless guys who would wander in off the streets of Nashville just to get warm inside the dive where he was playing.

"I played five or six nights a week if I could get it, four hours minimum for five dollars an hour and tips," Chesney said in an interview on GACTV.com online. "When you're making music in Music City, it's all okay."

Looking out over those thousands of screaming fans in Pittsburgh, with TV cameras all around, Chesney had to

One of Chesney's dreams was to live near the ocean, a place that has always given him peace. Once his dreams came true, wearing a shell necklace from the islands became his trademark.

remind himself it was no longer a dream. He was living the dream! The small-town boy from East Tennessee whose favorite food is macaroni and cheese had finally made it to the very top. He was a superstar.

Still, on the inside, he knew he was the same small-town boy — with big dreams and a big heart. Those things are what brought him to this historic concert in Pittsburgh, and those things will carry him throughout his life. That heart and those dreams are why Kenny Chesney isn't going away any time soon.

Getting Started

Kenneth Arnold Chesney came into this world on March 26, 1968, at St. Mary's Hospital in Knoxville, Tennessee, but he was raised in a nearby small town named Luttrell—best known as the hometown of Chet Atkins. Luttrell only had about 915 people in it when Kenny was born. It was and still is the kind of place where everybody knows everybody. No one knew Kenny Chesney yet, but one day they would.

His parents, Karen (Chandler) and David Chesney, had no idea their precious baby boy would one day become a big country music star. He just seemed like an ordinary kid—getting dirty and having nonstop fun. Later, Kenny's parents had another child, Jennifer, and Kenny had a baby sister for a playmate. She always called her brother "Buh," short for "Bubba." But Kenny's family didn't stay together for long. Karen and Dave divorced when Kenny was just a toddler.

With Karen making little money as a hairstylist, Kenny learned to entertain himself on a budget. He didn't even own a baseball or a bat growing up. He would just pick up rocks from the driveway and hit them with a broom handle. Sometimes he would chill out inside the house, watching his grandparents' black-and-white television set. Karen got help raising Kenny and his sister from extended family—her parents, her sister, the kids' father, and her new husband. Kenny and his sister were constantly surrounded by love.

Kenny also had a love for music. Karen and her twin sister, Sharon, used to sing gospel music all around East Tennessee. They were known as the Grigsby Twins, and their dad (Kenny's grandpa) used to haul them everywhere to sing. You might say singing was in Kenny's blood. It's no wonder Kenny liked music so much.

As a boy, he listened to both country and rock and roll. One of his favorite Christmas presents he ever received was the *Elvis Presley Double Live* album. He was only six years old at the time, but Kenny knew good music when he heard it.

> "I used to sit with a hairbrush in front of a mirror and pretend that I was Elvis."

"I listened to that album over and over again," he said in an interview with *American Profile*. "I used to sit with a hairbrush in front of a mirror and pretend that I was Elvis. Because it was a live album, I pretended the applause was for me."

Kenny liked music, but he didn't get serious about making music until he was in college. He was too busy doing

Chesney and his mother, Karen Chandler, pose together at the 33rd Annual Academy of Country Music Awards in April 1997. Chandler grew up singing gospel music with her sister, so Chesney gets some of his musical abilities from her. They share a love for each other and for great music.

the stuff other boys in his small town did—mostly, playing sports.

"I grew up in a very small town, went to a small elementary, then high school—and got to play football as a starter," he said, noting that he may have been the slowest, smallest receiver in the history of high school football.

Still, he made the team and worked hard enough to stay on it. That's pretty much how Chesney has lived his whole life, especially when it comes to his music career. Unlike many of today's country music stars, Chesney didn't hit it big in the beginning. He had to work very hard, pay his dues, and believe in himself.

After graduating from Gibbs High School in 1987, Kenny entered college at East Tennessee State University. That year for Christmas, he received a guitar. It was the perfect present because it brought out the musical gift inside him. He started dreaming big. He could see himself in front of thousands of screaming fans. He could picture it in his mind.

In reality, he was learning to play live music in small settings. First, he played with the college's bluegrass band. Next, he played five nights a week for tips at a little place called Chucky's Trading Post in Johnson City. He was a student by day and a struggling musician by night. Chesney practiced hard at his music—sometimes as much as seven

Unlike many of today's country music stars, Chesney didn't hit it big in the beginning.

hours a day. Sure it was a lot of work, but he had no problem with hard work. He knew that he would have to work even harder to make it as a country singer, because the odds were not in his favor. Garth Brooks, Vince Gill, Clint Black, and Alan Jackson were dominating the country music scene at that time, and Chesney knew he would have to live, sleep, eat, and breathe country music if he was going to compete with those guys.

He had such a following that he eventually sold 1,000 copies of a self-released demo album filled with songs he'd written.

"I made up my mind I was going to figure out how to make my living playing music," he said in an interview with GACTV.com online.

And that's what he did. Meanwhile he gained confidence in his abilities. He also played at Quarterback's Barbecue in Johnson City. If they were paying, he was playing. He fit right in with the locals. They liked their country music real and raw, and that's the only way Chesney knew how to play it.

"The scene up there then was mostly blues, rock and folk," he said in an interview on CMT.com online. "I was about the only one doing George Jones and Hank Jr. I got to where I had a pretty good following."

In fact, he had such a following that he eventually sold 1,000 copies of a self-released demo album filled with songs he'd written. He made this album in the Classic Recording Studio in Bristol, Virginia, along with several musicians he knew from college. (Those guys are now part of Alison Krauss' band.)

He knew that if he was going to go for his dreams, Nashville would be the place to do it. With the money he earned from selling those 1,000 records, he was able to purchase a Martin guitar. After Chesney graduated with a marketing degree in 1991, he took his guitar and headed for Nashville.

Chesney ended up performing at the Turf, which was a rough honky-tonk place in a rundown part of the city. He played and played and sang and sang—night after night. He gained lots of experience, but he knew that the Turf wasn't the kind of place you get discovered. However, he did have a bad little tape recording of his musical abilities that a friend had dubbed for him. Chesney gave it to Clay Bradley, who worked for BMI at the time. Bradley made sure that poor-quality little tape found its way into the right hands.

That was a lucky break for Chesney, because he was given the chance to audition with the Opryland Music Group.

That was a lucky break for Chesney, because he was given the chance to audition with the Opryland Music Group. He left that audition with a songwriter's contract and a big smile on his face. It was 1992, and he was on his way, but the road leading to his dreams would have a few rest stops and detours along the way.

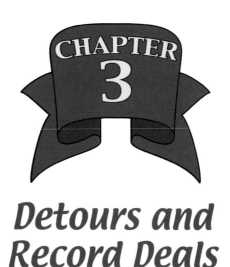

Detours and Record Deals

Several months later, Chesney made an appearance at a songwriter's showcase, which proved to be a very good move: It led to a recording contract with Capricorn Records. As luck would have it, Capricorn had just started a country music division, and Chesney was the perfect country music singer to launch the company's new line. In 1993, his first real album was released. It was called *In My Wildest Dreams.*

With the album out, Chesney had high hopes for success, but only a few singles from it had made any waves when Capricorn closed its Nashville office. It seemed as if his career was over before it had really begun.

"It was one of those things where, looking back, it's hard to believe you didn't get discouraged or doubt," Chesney said in an interview with GACTV.com online. "But in the moment, it all felt like it was happening, because you didn't know what happening really was."

When Chesney became famous, he lost weight, started working out, and began wearing sleeveless shirts and tight jeans along with his famous black hat. His female fans went wild! They liked his new look.

Chesney never lost hope. Even though Capricorn closed, his song "The Tin Man" got some airplay. It only hit number 70 on the Billboard country singles chart, but that was enough to get the attention of Joe Galante of RCA. Galante called Chesney and offered him a contract, and that wasn't all. He also offered to buy the original recordings of Chesney's Capricorn album. It was an all-star day for Chesney and for country music.

Galante signed Chesney to RCA's sister label, BNA Records, which released the Capricorn album. It sold 100,000 copies.

Chesney knew he had more hit songs inside him. The executives at BNA Records believed in Chesney, too.

Chesney knew he had more hit songs inside him. The executives at BNA Records believed in Chesney, too.

In 1995, Chesney came out with *All I Need to Know*—his first original album with BNA Records. This one sold more than 300,000 copies. He was definitely on his way. *All I Need to Know* gave him his first two Top Ten hits—"All I Need to Know" and "Fall in Love."

In 1996, *Me And You* was released, and that album went gold. (For an album to go gold in the United States, it must sell at least 500,000 copies.) Two singles from that album went to number two on the charts. Those songs were "Me And You" and "When I Close My Eyes."

More people started liking this small-town singer from Tennessee. He didn't have the voice of Vince Gill or the charisma of Alan Jackson, but he had something very special.

Chesney insists that he's just like everybody else, but what sets him apart are his hard work and determination.

He was a guy everyone could relate to, and that worked for him.

"I think people realize that. I'm not so different from them, they hear it in the songs — and I'm like their buddy," Chesney once said. "You know, it's not a bad way to make friends."

Chesney was starting to make a lot of friends. He went from playing for twelve people in a rough nightclub in a scary part of town to selling out big arenas. He had survived the early setbacks, and now he was truly on the road to his destiny. He was walking in his dreams, but Chesney wasn't through dreaming.

Not yet . . .

Dreaming Bigger, Getting Rowdy

*C*hesney's dreams and his winning attitude kept the hits coming consistently.

In 1997, his *I Will Stand* went platinum. In 1999, *Everywhere We Go* went double platinum, which means it sold two million copies.

Chesney made the newspapers in the year 2000 not only for his great musical abilities and his sellout shows, but also for his rowdiness. He and Tim McGraw, another country music star, ran into a bit of trouble with the police in New York State. It seems that Chesney hopped on a police officer's horse at a fair and was irritated when the officer tried to pull him off. Chesney says he had permission to climb aboard the horse. Police reports said that Tim McGraw blocked the policeman's efforts to get Chesney down from his mount, so both men were in big trouble with the law. Chesney was charged with disorderly conduct, and McGraw was charged with obstructing governmental administration and resisting arrest. Both men were acquitted of those charges. The publicity that this "horsing around" stunt received turned out to be priceless. As they say in show business, there is no such thing as bad publicity.

Besides, those who know Chesney best know that he is a giving, caring person. Even early on, he was donating money to St. Jude Children's Research Hospital and the Make-A-Wish Foundation. And he has never forgotten the folks who helped him get started down the path toward his dreams.

> *Even early on, he was donating money to St. Jude Children's Research Hospital and the Make-A-Wish Foundation.*

"When I first moved to Nashville, I played four hours a night at a grungy bar called the Turf, which was then a hangout for the homeless," Chesney said in an interview with *USA Weekend.* "At first it was a little spooky, but you look past a dirty shirt and you can find a helluva guy. I wouldn't trade that experience for anything. I made my last will and testament in 2002, and a couple of the regulars at the Turf are in it."

In 2000, Chesney's *Greatest Hits* album reminded the world of his hit-after-hit track record. It sold more than 3 million copies. On the heels of that success, his *No Shoes, No Shirt, No Problems* album got lots of radio play in 2002, and it let his fans know of his love for the ocean, the islands, and life itself. It was a more serious side of Chesney, and the fans seemed to like it a lot.

"With 'No Shoes,' I think we had fun and looked at some pretty rough emotions," Chesney shared in an interview

Uncle Kracker, left, opened for Chesney during his Margaritas 'n Señoritas tour. He also performs with Chesney on the wildly popular duet "When the Sun Goes Down."

featured on his official website, www.kennychesney.com. "I'd like to think I'm serious enough to do a song like 'Some People Change' or 'When I Think About Leaving,' but am also the kind of guy who'd hang out in the islands with Uncle Kracker, the way 'When the Sun Goes Down' is. That's how people really are: both! They need and want that."

Chesney's Margaritas 'n Señoritas Tour in 2003 was historic. He sold more tickets than ever before, breaking attendance records at almost every venue he played. As if that weren't enough to make it a good year, Chesney also had the chance to headline a concert at Knoxville's mecca of football, University of Tennessee's Neyland Stadium—a great honor for a former high school football player.

"It took three days for my ears to stop ringing and the sound of the crowd cheering from that show to die out . . . ," he shared in an interview for BNA Records. "When you take the time to understand . . . you start to feel really honored that all these people spent their summer with you, brought their party to your show, told you how your songs were their life."

That 2003 tour connected Chesney to his fans in a way he'd never been before. He already had a great fan base, but that year he developed a loyal fan following. He also filmed a behind-the-scenes DVD in 2003, and he released the holiday album *All I Want for Christmas Is a Real Good Tan*. He had crossed over from being a rising star to a superstar.

> *Chesney also had the chance to headline a concert at Knoxville's mecca of football, University of Tennessee's Neyland Stadium.*

Loving, Winning, and Losing

*A*t the end of 2003, Kenny Chesney's "There Goes My Life" was at the top of the Billboard country singles chart. That was just a sampling of the success his new album, *When the Sun Goes Down*, would bring in 2004. This album sold 550,581 copies its first week, which immediately landed Chesney at number one on Billboard's top 200 overall and country album charts.

When the Sun Goes Down won a Country Music Association (CMA) Award, and Chesney won the CMA Entertainer of the Year trophy. He had made it to the top. The five-foot-six small-town guy in the cowboy hat with the sly smile had finally hit the big time, and now the entire world knew it.

Chesney wondered if life could get any better. The beginning of 2005 proved it could. That's when he met the girl of his dreams, Academy Award–winning actress Renée Zellweger. They met at NBC's Tsunami Relief Telethon, and there was an instant connection between them. Strangely enough, in 1999 Chesney had actually written a hit song,

Chesney performs for Tsunami Aid: A Concert of Hope. The fund-raiser would benefit victims of the 2004 tsunami in Indonesia.

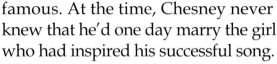

"You Had Me From Hello," after seeing the movie *Jerry Maguire.* In that successful movie, which featured Zellweger and Tom Cruise, Renée made the line "You had me at hello" famous. At the time, Chesney never knew that he'd one day marry the girl who had inspired his successful song.

After Kenny and Renée met, they kept in contact through cell phone calls and emails. When their busy careers allowed, they'd secretly get together for dates. It was a quick romance, but quite intense. On April 29, 2005, after months of secret calls, emails, and dates, Renée attended Kenny's concert in Jacksonville, Florida. As part of his show, she delivered a drink to him onstage, and the crowd went wild. That was their first public appearance as a couple.

Then on May 9, Kenny and Renée surprised everyone by getting married on tiny St. John in the Virgin Islands.

Then on May 9, Kenny and Renée surprised everyone by getting married on tiny St. John in the Virgin Islands. Pictures of the happy couple were everywhere, showing them barefoot on the beach in their wedding clothes. Of course, Kenny had on his cowboy hat. He was quoted as saying, "I am the luckiest man alive."

His good luck continued, because just a few days later, he won the title of Entertainer of the Year at the Academy of Country Music Awards in Las Vegas. This was a very big deal. Since he had already won the award for Top New Vocalist, Top Male Vocalist, and now Entertainer of the Year, he earned what the Academy of Country Music calls the Triple Crown, which honors artists who have won in all three (male or female) categories. In fact, he is one of only six other artists to win the Triple Crown. The others are Brooks & Dunn, the Dixie Chicks, Mickey Gilley, Merle Haggard, and Barbara Mandrell.

"Being one of such an amazing six pack makes you stop and think about everything country music means," Chesney shared in an interview posted on his official website. "It's one of those things that you go, 'ME?!' because, you know, there's still so much that I dream and want to accomplish."

After the ceremony, Kenny and Renée celebrated his great victory. They seemed as happy as they could be at the after-party. But there wasn't much time to spend together. Renée had to go on the road to promote her new movie, *Cinderella Man,* and Chesney went back to his concert tour. Finally on June 9, the couple was able to get together in Las Vegas for a five-day honeymoon.

On June 16, Chesney had the great honor of tossing out the first pitch at an Oakland A's baseball game.

On June 16, Chesney had the great honor of tossing out the first pitch at an Oakland A's baseball game, as Renée continued her movie's promotional tour. They found a few more days to spend together (July 28–30) before Chesney's July 30 concert in Pittsburgh, but then Renée flew back to her home in Connecticut—alone. This was really the beginning of the end. Kenny sensed that his marriage was in trouble, but he wasn't sure what to do about it.

On August 28, Chesney finished his concert tour in Louisville, Kentucky, and headed to his home on St. John, without his wife. The ocean has always been a retreat for Chesney — a place where he can think more clearly and rest in private. On September 5, Renée kicked off the overseas promotion of *Cinderella Man* at the Venice Film Festival, all alone. On September 14, she shocked their fans by filing for an annulment of their marriage. (An annulment is different from a divorce. A divorce ends a marriage, while an annulment means the marriage was never legally valid.)

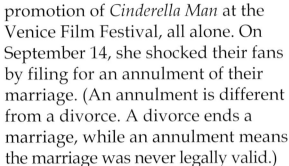

The ocean has always been a retreat for Chesney—a place where he can think more clearly.

One of the biggest celebrity marriages of the year had ended after only four months. Once Renée released a statement about her decision to file for an annulment, Kenny spoke out.

"I'm all right," he told *Country Weekly* magazine. "There have been better times, but I'll be OK."

At age thirty-seven, Kenny had lost loves before. He has talked of his high school sweetheart breaking his heart, and there have been others. Like always, Chesney will learn from this hardship and then write about it in his heartfelt songs.

"I need a break real bad, and I'm going to go away for a couple of weeks," he added. "I'll be fine. I'm tired right now, but by next year, I'll be excited to get back to it. And it'll be about the music again, not about the sideshow" (referring to the constant press coverage of his romance with Renée).

For Kenny Chesney, it's always been about the music, and it always will be. And, if he can find a way to help people along the way, he is happy to oblige.

Besides relaxing on the beach, Chesney will take a break by playing a few rounds of golf.

On November 8, 2005, Chesney's CD *The Road and the Radio* went on sale at JCPenney stores across the United States. Charitable Chesney and BNA Records joined forces with the department store chain to help kids. JCPenney promised to donate all of its net profits from the CD, and BNA would donate a percentage of November sales of the CD, to the JCPenney Afterschool Fund.

"There are 15 million kids who are home alone in the afternoons without any adult guidance or supervision, and that can lead to a lot of problems. So JCPenney and I are doing something about it," Chesney said in a press release posted on his website.

To further promote this worthy project, Chesney performed during the national broadcast of the Thanksgiving Day Parade that aired on CBS before heading home to his mama's house for the holidays.

His good deeds have definitely paid off. His single, "Who You'd Be Today" from *The Road and the Radio* became the fastest growing chart hit of his career. And that album sold just fewer than 269,000 units for the week ending December 25, hitting number two on the charts.

Chesney doesn't know what the future will hold for him personally and professionally, but he is ready for whatever life brings him. After experiencing great success over the past few years, he is truly a superstar. Still, his fans think of him as the superstar next door. No matter how successful he becomes, he will always stay true to his country roots and loyal to the fans who put him at the top.

No matter how successful he becomes, he will always stay true to his country roots and loyal to his fans.

"Where I'm from, no matter what you listen to, you talk country, you think country, you are country," he shared on his official website. "Your family's country. The food on your table's country. The church you go to on Sunday morning's country. . . . And that's a good thing. It means something. It stands for something. And, truly, when you scrape it all away, that is who I am."

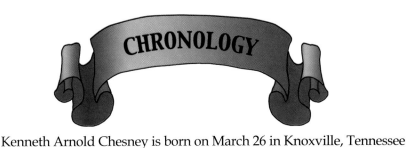

CHRONOLOGY

1968 Kenneth Arnold Chesney is born on March 26 in Knoxville, Tennessee

1987 Graduates from Gibbs High School

1990 Graduates from East Tennessee State University in Johnson City with a degree in advertising and marketing

1991 Auditions for Opryland Music Group, landing a songwriter's contract

1995 *All I Need to Know* (his debut BNA album) sells more than 300,000 copies

1996 *Me and You* is certified gold

1997 *I Will Stand* is certified platinum

1999 *Everywhere We Go* is certified double platinum

2000 Chesney and country superstar Tim McGraw have a run-in with the law for hopping on a police officer's horse

2001 *Greatest Hits* sells more than 3 million copies

2002 *No Shoes, No Shirt, No Problems* lands him in the big leagues; *People* magazine names him one of the sexiest men alive

2003 Embarks on an extremely successful tour, makes a behind-the-scenes DVD, and releases the holiday album *All I Want for Christmas Is a Real Good Tan*

2004 *When the Sun Goes Down* wins a CMA Award, and Chesney wins the CMA Entertainer of the Year trophy

2005 January, releases *Be As You Are*
January 15, meets Renée Zellweger at NBC's Tsunami Relief Telethon and sparks fly . . .
April 29, Kenny and Renée go public with their love affair at his concert in Jacksonville, Florida
May 9, Kenny and Renée get married on tiny St. John; Kenny says, "I'm the luckiest man alive"
May 17, Chesney wins Entertainer of the Year at the Academy of Country Music Awards in Las Vegas
September 14, Renée files for an annulment of their marriage
November 8, Chesney releases *The Road and the Radio*
November 23, Chesney stars in his first network TV special, *Somewhere in the Sun*

2006 "Who You'd Be Today" becomes the fastest growing chart hit of his career; Pollstar.com ranks Margaritas 'n Señoritas the seventh top-grossing tour of 2005 for all genres; the first date for *The Road and the Radio* concert sells out in four minutes

AWARDS

2005	Academy of Country Music: Entertainer of the Year
	United Stations Networks: Most Successful Artist in Country Music
2004	Country Music Association (CMA) Award: Album of the Year (*When the Sun Goes Down*)
	CMA Award: Entertainer of the Year
	Country Music Television (CMT) Flameworthy Video Music Award: Hottest Video of the Year
	CMT Flameworthy Video Music Award: Male Video of the Year
2003	Academy of Country Music: Single of the Year ("The Good Stuff")
	Academy of Country Music: Top Male Vocalist
2002	CMT Flameworthy Video Music Awards: Male Video of the Year
	CMT Flameworthy Video Music Awards: Video of the Year
	Billboard Country Single of the Year ("The Good Stuff")
1997	Academy of Country Music: Top New Male Vocalist

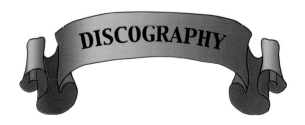

DISCOGRAPHY

Albums

2005	*The Road and the Radio*
	Be As You Are: Songs From an Old Blue Chair
2004	*When the Sun Goes Down*
2003	*All I Want for Christmas Is a Real Good Tan*
2002	*No Shoes, No Shirt, No Problems*
2000	*Greatest Hits*
1999	*Everywhere We Go*
1997	*I Will Stand*
1996	*Me and You*
1995	*All I Need to Know*
	In My Wildest Dreams (re-released in 2004)

Career-Defining Singles

2005	"Who You'd Be Today"
2004	"When the Sun Goes Down"
	"I Go Back"
2003	"There Goes My Life"
	"No Shoes, No Shirt, No Problems"

For Young Adults

Adelman, Kim. "The Girls' Guide to Country: The Music, the Hunks, the Hair, the Clothes and More!" *Broadway,* October 14, 2003.

Agamaite, Jenny. "Kenny Chesney Concert in Wisconsin." March 23, 2005.
http://www.wisconsin-music.com/articles/reviews/kenny-chesney

Chesney, Kenny. *No Shoes, No Shirt, No Problems.* (Songbook.) Hal Leonard Corporation, October 1, 2002.

Chesney, Kenny. *When the Sun Goes Down.* (Songbook.) Hal Leonard Corporation, June 1, 2004.

Countryfans.net: Kenny Chesney
http://countryfans.net/articles/shel/kennyfacts.shtml

Gordinier, Jeff. Men.style.com. "Kenny Chesney."
http://men.style.com/details/features/landing?id=content_2102

Works Consulted

AOL Music: "Kenny Chesney"
http://music.aol.com/artist/main.adp?tab=main&artistid=64127&albumid=0

Artist Spotlight: "Kenny Chesney"
http://groups.msn.com/CountryMusicRow/kennychesney.msnw

Bonaguro, Alison. "Kenny Chesney Makes Farm Aid Debut."
http://www.cmt.com/artists/news/1509879/09192005/chesney_kenny.jhtml

"Chesney Crew" — #1 Fansite
http://www.chesneycrew.com/

CMT.com. Kenny Chesney Biography.
www.cmt.com/artists/az/chesney_kenny/bio.jhtml

Haislop, Neil. "Kenny Chesney . . . Ascending to the Top Ranks." Great American Country.
http://www.gactv.com/MeetTheStars/kchesney0304.html

Keel, Beverly. "Kenny Chesney's Christmas." American Profile. December 11–15, 2005.
http://www.americanprofile.com/issues/20031214/20031214_3551.asp

Kenny Chesney Lyrics: "I Go Back"
http://www.azlyrics.com/lyrics/kennychesney/igoback.html

"Kenny Chesney — No Shirt, No Shoes, No Problems." Great American Country.
www.gactv.com/artists/chesney.html

Kenny Chesney Official Website
http://www.kennychesney.com/home.php

Rolling Stone.com.
"Kenny Chesney." http://www.rollingstone.com/artists/43391/biography

VH1.com.
"Kenny Chesney" http://www.vh1.com/artists/az/chesney_kenny/artist.jhtml

INDEX